GARY JONES

Savannah

First edition

Contents

Introduction

This book contains a definitive guide about touring Savannah in the best way possible.

Known as the Hostess City of the South, Savannah is one of the oldest cities in the United States. It is further made famous by being featured in high-profile films—such as "Forrest Gump" starring Tom Hanks, Sally Field, and Robin Wright—as well by the best-selling non-fiction book entitled "Midnight in the Garden of Good and Evil".

Technically, there is no right or wrong way to tour Savannah. It would depend on your preferences after all. However, it would not hurt your budget, time, and effort to learn more about the city that you are going to visit.

To help you come up with a suitable travel itinerary for your trip to Savannah, this book would help you:

- Better appreciate the history and background of Savannah;
- Learn the best times of the year to go visit Savannah;
- Figure out what things to pack in your suitcase based on the expected weather in the city throughout the year;
- Keep yourself safe while exploring the city;
- Find out the best ways to get in and out of Savannah;
- Learn more about the various ways to go around the city;
- Discover the best yet affordable places to stay at while touring Savannah;
- Find out the top 5 restaurants in the city, the best time to go dine there, and which menu item you should try out;
- Learn more about the most iconic landmarks of the city;
- Explore the best Savannah museums that would help understand better the history and culture of the city;
- Discover your new favorite artists by browsing through the best art galleries of Savannah;
- Find out the best coffee shops in the city, when you should hang out there, and which beverages and dishes you should give a try;
- Spend the evening at the best Savannah bars;
- Get your blood pumping by showing you the top 5 night clubs in the city; and
- Discover the fun and unique things you can do while exploring Savannah.

As an added bonus, a sample 3-day travel itinerary shall also be provided in this book for your reference. Go through the suggested list of places to visit, restaurants to dine at, and fun things to do during your brief stay at the city.

If you find it exciting and interesting, then go ahead, and schedule your trip. Otherwise, feel free to customize the itinerary according to your preferences and what you would learn from each chapter of this book.

Thanks for downloading this book, I hope you enjoy it!

1

Brief History and Background

As the oldest city of the US state of Georgia, Savannah has a rich and colorful history that all started back in 1733. Hundreds of years later, Savannah continues to uphold its reputation as one of the most beautiful and vibrant cities of the South.

The Founding of Savannah

Aboard the ship named "Anne", General James Oglethorpe, along with 120 passengers, landed in the banks of the Savannah River. Finding the land to be suitable for a settlement, he claimed it as the 13th colony of England in America.

Gen. Oglethorpe named the surrounding lands as "Georgia" in honor of the King George II of England, and declared Savannah as its first city. He did not waste time in planning out the city according to a specific set of rules. Through Gen. Oglethorpe's careful survey of the land, he had managed to divide the city of Savannah into a series of grids. This layout led to the creation of wide streets and several public squares—22 of which continues to exist up to this day.

The Value of Savannah throughout History

After a few decades, Savannah had been proven to be more than just a planned city. During the American Revolution and the American Civil War, Savannah was home to one of the strategic ports that both sides of each war had tried to control.

Furthermore, due to the rich soil and optimal climate of Savannah, plantation owners constructed several cotton fields and rice fields across the city. As a result, the slavery system had flourished at the time, turning the city into a commercial port.

The economic dependence of the city on slaves reached a critical point during the Civil War. As a port, Savannah suffered greatly from the sea blockades, which ultimately crushed its economy. Soon after, it was reclaimed by General William Sherman of the Union Army as a present to President Abraham Lincoln. As the legend goes, Gen. Sherman was awestruck by the beauty of Savannah that he could not bring himself to burn it along with the other Southern cities he had captured.

Today, Savannah remains to be one of the major cities in the United States of America. Given its long and storied past, the city has established itself as a strong industrial center, a strategic seaport, and cultural hub.

The old beauty and historical significance of Savannah have also turned it into one of the most frequently visited tourist spots in the Southern US. Its appeal is further enhanced by the city's brand of hospitality. As such, it should not come as a surprise that more than 50 million people have visited Savannah in the last 10 years.

2

Best Time to Go, and Weather and Safety in the City

If you want to see Savannah at its best, schedule your trip to the city between the months of March and July. During this period, the warm weather is just right for the tree leaves and flower blooms to awaken from hibernation.

Several major festivals and public celebrations are also held during this season:

- St. Patrick's Day Celebrations (mid-March)
- Savannah Music Festival (March or April)
- Sidewalk Arts Festival (April)
- SCAD (or the Savannah College of Art and Design) Sand Arts Festival (May)
- River Street Seafood Fest (May or June)
- Fourth of July on the Waterfront (July)

Because your trip would likely be jam-packed with events and sights that are unique to the city, expect that the hotel rates would be higher than average during these months as well.

If you are on a tight budget, however, you should go to Savannah during the months of January and February. Remember to pack accordingly because you would be going to the city in late winter.

This period is considered as the low season of the Savannah, so expect the city to be more subdued and less crowded than during the spring and early summer seasons. Case in point, the Black Heritage Festival held every February is usually the only big event that is publicly celebrated in the city. Most hotels also offer huge discounts and packages, so be sure to research carefully to get the best deals for you.

For those seeking for something in between, the ideal time to go to Savannah is from the month of September to November. At this point, most of the summer crowds are beginning to disperse. Expect the weather to be cooler, too, given that fall has most likely started by September.

You may also take part in the following celebrations and big festivals held during these months:

- Savannah Jazz Fest (September)
- Savannah Pride Festival (mid to late October)
- SCAD (or the Savannah College of Art and Design) Savannah Film Festival (October to November)
- Savannah Food and Wine Festival (early November)
- Savannah Harbor Boat Parade of Lights (late November)

Since there is a dip in the number of tourists during these months, hotel prices tend to be lower than average, too. Many hotels also offer special packages to attract more visitors before the holiday season begins.

Savannah Monthly Weather

January

Though winter is at its peak during this month, snow rarely falls in Savannah. Some January evenings would feel icy though because this is the coldest month of the year in the city.

Average Temperature Range: 38.1 to 59.7 0F (3.4 to 15.4 0C)
Average Precipitation: 3.59 inches (9.1 centimeters)

February

The weather is a little less chilly, and a bit dryer during this month. Therefore, you should still bring along with you your favorite cold weather gear.

- Average Temperature Range: 41.2 to 62.4 0F (5.1 to 16.9 0C)
- Average Precipitation: 3.2 inches (8.2 centimeters)

March

Springtime in Savannah begins in March. Even though the temperature has risen up by several degrees, you may still have to wear thick sweaters or cardigans during the evenings.

- Average Temperature Range: 48.4 to 70.2 0F (9.1 to 21.2 0C)
- Average Precipitation: 3.8 inches (9.6 centimeters)

April

The weather in April brings forth the full bloom of the flowers in Savannah. Most of the foliage has also re-emerged, thus making this month the best time to go for walking tours around the scenic city.

- Average Temperature Range: 54.5 to 77.5 0F (12.5 to 25.3 0C)
- Average Precipitation: 3 inches (7.7 centimeters)

May

During this month, you may still enjoy the last few weeks of spring in Savannah. Unlike early and mid-spring, the temperatures in May are on the more comfortable side of the season.

- Average Temperature Range: 63 to 84 0F (17.2 to 28.9 0C)
- Average Precipitation: 4 inches (10.4 centimeters)

June

Savannah summer usually starts in June. At this point, the temperature will gradually rise up day by day, so make sure to bring some light clothes with you.

- Average Temperature Range: 69.3 to 88.9 0F (20.7 to 31.6 0C)
- Average Precipitation: 5.7 inches (14.4 centimeters)

July

Heat in Savannah reaches its peak by mid-July. Expect this month to be sweltering and humid.

- Average Temperature Range: 72.3 to 91 0F (22.4 to 32.8 0C)
- Average Precipitation: 6.4 inches (16.2 centimeters)

August

The city heat slightly subsides in August, mainly due to the more frequent rainfall during this month. Remember to pack an umbrella and maybe a pair of rain boots, too.

- Average Temperature Range: 72.1 to 89.8 0F (22.3 to 32.1 0C)
- Average Precipitation: 7.5 inches (18.9 centimeters)

September

The transition to fall begins in September. Therefore, the temperature will steadily decline, along with a significant drop in the frequency of rainy days.

- Average Temperature Range: 67.8 to 85.3 0F (19.9 to 29.6 0C)
- Average Precipitation: 4.5 inches (11.4 centimeters)

October

Fall weather is in its full swing by October. If you enjoy looking at autumnal colors, then visit Savannah during this time to go sight-seeing across the 22 public squares in the city.

- Average Temperature Range: 56.8 to 77.5 0F (13.8 to 25.3 0C)
- Average Precipitation: 2.4 inches (6.1 centimeters)

November

As the last of the fall months, November marks the start of significant drops in temperature. This also happens to be the driest month in Savannah.

- Average Temperature Range: 48 to 70 0F (8.9 to 21.1 0C)
- Average Precipitation: 2.2 inches (5.6 centimeters)

December

Winter officially begins in December for Savannah. The temperature would continue to decrease with each day, thus making this the second coldest month of the year.

- Average Temperature Range: 41 to 62.2 0F (5 to 16.8 0C)
- Average Precipitation: 2.9 inches (7.5 centimeters)

Safety in the City

Though Savannah is known for being the epitome of Southern charm and hospitality, you should still be mindful of the possible dangers that are lurking across the city.

· **Criminals**

Like most popular tourist destinations, one of the greatest dangers that may threaten your safety are criminals of all kinds. Certain areas of the city are hot spots for thieves and muggers. This especially applies to streets that are lined with bars because you might also have to navigate your way through a throng of rowdy, drunk people.

Be extra mindful of where you keep your cash. Stay away from darkened corners, where only a few people pass by. If you are driving, double-check the locks of your car to ensure the security of both your car, and any personal belongings that you have left there.

Avoid going south of Forsyth Park, too. These areas are not known for being hospitable to tourists, unlike the areas near Historic District.

· **Food Safety**

Check out the reviews of a restaurant before choosing to dine in there. You would not want a case of food poisoning to ruin your stay in Savannah. Be wary because high prices do not necessarily equate to good and safe food. Read through the experiences of other people to keep yourself from making an avoidable mistake.

- **Redbugs**

Many trees in Savannah have Spanish Moss hanging on their branches. Though they are beautiful to look at, you should steer clear from the Spanish Moss. They are home to the redbugs, which can pierce through your skin, and cause irritation and pain.

· **Steep Staircases**

Because of the prevailing architectural design in the city, you should be extra careful when ascending or descending the stairs in certain tourist spots. This particularly applies to those locations near the River Street.

To keep yourself from a nasty tumble down the stairs, use an elevator whenever possible. Otherwise, take your time when using the stairs.

All in all, just try to keep a sharp eye and an alert mind while travelling around the city. Use your common sense when interacting with both the locals and other tourists. If you are not sure about where you are heading, hail or book a cab rather than risk getting lost in the streets of Savannah.

3

Transport

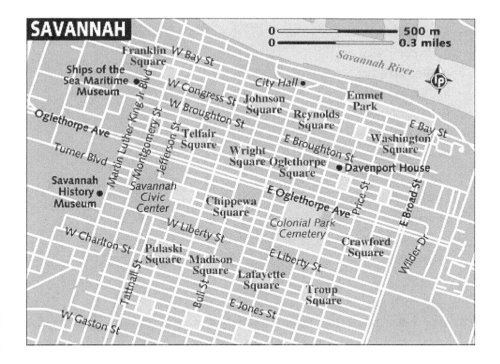

There are four basic ways to get to Savannah, Georgia. You may also consider these options when you are about to leave the city.

1 - Take a flight to the city.

This is the quickest, albeit not the cheapest, among the three options. The primary airport that serves the city is the Savannah/Hilton Head (SAV) International Airport. It is located near downtown Savannah, thus making it easier for you to reach several key tourist spots in the city.

The airport services both domestic and international flights of several major airline companies, including:

- Air Canada
- Aeromexico
- Air France
- American Airlines
- All Nippon Airways
- JetBlue Airways
- British Airways
- Delta Air Lines
- Frontier Airlines
- KLM Royal Dutch Airlines
- United Airlines Korean Air
- Lufthansa Airline
- Singapore Airlines
- Qatar Airways
- Korean Air

The expected airfare varies depending on the timing of your trip, among other factors. If you want to get the best deals, it is best to book your flight a couple of months in advance.

2 - Drive to the city

Many visitors to Savannah find it easy to get there by car. For those who wants to take a practical route, the I-95 (or Interstate 95) lies 10 miles to the West of Savannah. Other common routes that you may opt to drive through includes the I-16, U.S. Route 17, and U.S. Route 80 of the national highway system.

On the other hand, some travelers prefer going through a more scenic route by flying in to Atlanta, and starting their drive there to Savannah. Along the way, they will pass by Macon, a county in Georgia that is home to numerous historical and cultural sites. They will also be passing by a series of large, moss-draped trees, and houses that feature the iconic Southern architecture.

Once the trip around the city is over, a stopover at Tybee Island near the east coast is highly recommended before heading back to Atlanta, Georgia.

3 - Ride a bus to the city

Most of the buses going to and from coming Savannah are operated either by Greyhound or Southeastern Stages. Buses from both companies are equipped with power outlets and Wi-Fi connection. Advanced booking is recommended to guarantee good seats in your preferred spot.

4 - Board the train to the city.

Amtrak, a nation-wide passenger railroad service, operates a terminal in Savannah. At the moment, however, the route of the trains that passes through here is from Miami, Florida to New York, New York. If you live near the stop points of this route, then this may be the best option for you.

Going Around the City

In general, the public transport system in Savannah is made up of two components:

- **Downtown Transportation System (dot)**

Dot Website
  https://www.connectonthedot.com/

Established as a solution to the congested streets of central Savannah, this system is comprised of three separate transportation services whose routes go around the Historic District.

All three dot services may be used for free by anyone within the city. They are also accessible for people with disabilities.

For your reference, here are the free transportation services under the dot system:

Savannah Belles FerryJuliette Gordon Low, Florence Martus, Mary Musgrave, and Susie King Taylor, the four most influential women in the history of the city—this passenger ferry connects the Hutchinson Island to the River Street.

In total, there are 3 landing spots for the ferry:

- **Trade Center Landing**

Location: In between the Westin Hotel and the Trade Center on Hutchinson Island

Operations: Daily from 07:10 AM to 12:20 AM

- **Waving Girl Landing**

Location: River Walk near the Marriott Savannah Riverfront Hotel
   Operations: Daily from 08:20 AM to 06:30 PM

- **City Hall Landing**

Location: River Walk, behind the Savannah City Hall, and near the Hyatt Regency Savannah Hotel
   Operations: Daily from 07:00 AM to 12:30 AM

The ferry runs every 20 to 30 minutes during its operational hours. Through this, you may cross the river within 10 to 20 minutes, depending on the landings that would be covered by your trip.

Take note that announced and unannounced service interruptions may occur due to inclement weather, whenever there is too much fog in the river, or when a larger vessel is traversing up or down the river.

- **Express Shuttle – Downtown Route**

Use this service if you are heading somewhere in the upper Historic District. From there, the route is connected to the Martin Luther King, Jr. Boulevard, and Liberty Street. Take note that this route is looping in a clockwise fashion. With a total of 24 stops, you would be able to visit several public squares and other popular Savannah attractions, such as the Ships of the Sea Museum, City Market, Harper Fowlkes House, and the Savannah Theater.

- **Express Shuttle – Forsyth Park Route**

Taking a counter-clockwise route, this shuttle service forms a loop through the Bull Street, up to Drayton Street, and then down into the Whitaker Street. Aside from Forsyth Park itself, the 24 stops of this route would take you to several tourist destinations including the Georgia Historical Society, Telfair Museum of Art, and Jepson Center.

For your reference, here is the schedule followed by both Express Shuttle Routes.

- Monday to Friday – 07:00 AM to 12:00 MN
- Saturday – 10:00 AM to 12:00 MN
- Sunday – 10:00 AM to 09:00 PM
- Holidays – 10:00 AM to 09:00 PM

Take note that neither route operates during New Year's Day, Thanksgiving Day, and Christmas Day.

To board either of these shuttle services, you must wait for it to arrive at the designated bus stops marked with purple "dot" signposts. The average waiting time of each shuttle is 10 minutes per stop. Factor that in if you are going to use this service as your main means of travelling around the city.

- **Chatham Area Transit Bus Services**

If you are traveling beyond the Historic District, then you may use the services of the Chatham Area Transit (CAT). One of the most useful routes they have is the 100X Airport Express, which would take you directly to the SAV International Airport.

CAT has more than 60 buses that follow 20 routes around Savannah. You may board one by:

- Referring to the real-time bus information of the dedicated CAT app;
- Using the Google Trip Planner; or
- Using the CAT system map posted on its official website.

If you are traveling with your pet, you can board the Savannah Belles Ferry, but not any of the Express Shuttle or CAT buses. Exemption to this rule is given to service animals.

The best way to travel with a pet is to drive a car. Some cabs and ride-hailing services also allow animals.

Take note that driving around the city can be quite a challenge. The prevailing one-way system in most areas of the city creates congestion, especially near popular tourist spots.

Furthermore, it can hard to find a parking spot, particularly in the Historic District. You may then have to leave your car outside such areas to prevent any difficulties later on.

For these reasons, many tourists consider Savannah as a walking city. Fortunately, the frequently visited places are located near one another. Just be sure to wear your favorite walking shoes so that you can enjoy the city without ending up with sore feet.

If you are not keen about walking around the city, then you may consider joining a private bus tour instead. You can find one near the Visitors' Center and in selected areas of the Historic District.

For the more adventurous travelers, horse and carriage rides are pretty common in the Historic District as well. This would allow you to take in the scenery at a leisurely pace.

Try out the various means of getting around the city to get the full Savannah experience. As an extra precautionary measure, make sure to bring a map with you, even if you have joined a tour group.

4

Top 5 Affordable Hotels

Selecting the right hotel for you depends on your requirements as a traveler, and the areas you wish to visit while you are in Savannah. To help you decide where to stay at during your trip, here are the top 5 hotels that would surely fit your budget.

DoubleTree by Hilton Hotel Savannah

411 W Bay St, Savannah, GA 31401, United States
Phone: +1 912-790-7000

Get a first taste of Southern hospitality by being welcomed by the friendly hotel staff with freshly baked cookies. You can further explore what the city has to offer by staying in this hotel that is conveniently located in between the City Market and River Street.

Highly Rated Amenities:

- On-Site and Secured Parking
- Free Wi-Fi in All Areas of the Hotel
- Family Rooms
- Swimming Pool
- Hot Tub with Jacuzzi
- Non-Smoking Rooms
- Fully Equipped Bar
- Library

Closest Airport:

- Savannah/Hilton Head International Airport (6.6 miles or 11.2 km away)

Nearby Landmarks and Tourist Spots:

- Franklin Square (0.06 miles or 0.1 km away)
- Ships of the Sea Museum (0.1 miles or 0.2 km away)
- City Market (0.1 miles or 0.2 km away)
- Telfair Museum of Art (0.2 miles or 0.4 km away)

- Forsyth Park (0.2 miles or 0.4 km away)

Policy on Pets:

- An animal pet of any kind is not allowed inside the hotel.

Hyatt Place – Savannah Airport

4 Stephen S Green Dr, Savannah, GA 31408, United States
  Phone: +1 912-966-0020

Staying at this pet-friendly hotel would enable you to enjoy the city with your whole family in tow. Furthermore, its close proximity to the airport allows you to have more time to rest before heading off to your next destination.

Highly Rated Amenities:

- Free Airport Pick-Up and Drop-Off
- Express Check-In and Check-Out Service
- Free Wi-Fi in All Areas of the Hotel
- Swimming Pool
- Vending Machines for Drinks and Snacks
- Designated Smoking Area
- Family Rooms

Closest Airport:

- Savannah/Hilton Head International Airport (2.0 miles or 3.2 km away)

Nearby Landmarks and Tourist Spots:

- Crosswinds Golf Club (0.3 miles or 0.5 km away)
- Tanger Outlet Savannah (1.5 miles or 2.4 km away)
- Surf Lagoon Water Park (1.7 miles or 2.8 km away)
- Fun Zone Amusement and Sports Park (3.3 miles or 5.35 km away)
- Traffic Circle Shopping Center (6.1 miles or 9.8 km away)

Policy on Pets:

- For a certain charge, pets may be allowed to stay in the hotel upon request of the guest.

TRYP by Wyndham Savannah

320 Montgomery St, Savannah, GA 31401, United States
   Phone : +1 912-921-5300

Explore the city while staying at one of its trendiest hotels. Perfectly situated in the Historic district, you can out for a stroll, and reach popular tourist destinations in a matter of minutes.

Highly Rated Amenities:

- Express Check-In and Check-Out Service
- Luggage Storage
- On-Site Restaurant
- Free Wi-Fi in All Areas of the Hotel
- Safety Deposit Box
- Gym

- Fitness Center
- Designated Smoking Area
- Bar

Closest Airport:

- Savannah/Hilton Head International Airport (7.1 miles or 11.4 km away)

Nearby Landmarks and Tourist Spots:

- Pulaski Square (0.1 miles or 0.2 km away)
- Roundhouse Railroad Museum (0.2 miles or 0.3 km away)
- Green Meldrim House (0.2 miles or 0.3 km away)
- Ralph Mark Gilbert Civil Rights Museum (0.24 miles or 0.4 km away)
- The Mercer Williams House Museum (0.24 miles or 0.4 km away)

Policy on Pets:

- Guests may not bring their pets inside the hotel.

Fairfield Inn & Suites by Marriott Savannah

5801 Abercorn St, Savannah, GA 31405, United States
  Phone: +1 912-298-0800

Strategically located in the cultural center of Savannah, this hotel is rec-ommended for those who are planning to go on walking tours around the museums, art galleries, and public squares of the city.

Highly Rated Amenities:

- Secured Parking
- Charging Station for Electronic Vehicle
- Free Wi-Fi in All Areas of the Hotel
- Soundproof Rooms
- Safety Deposit Box
- Non-Smoking Rooms
- Bar
- Swimming Pool
- Outdoor Fireplace
- On-Site Mini Market

Closest Airport:

- Savannah/Hilton Head International Airport (6.9 miles or 11.1 km away)

Nearby Landmarks and Tourist Spots:

- Flame of Freedom (0.06 miles or 0.1 km away)
- Ships of the Sea Museum (0.1 miles or 0.2 km away)
- Telfair Museum of Art (0.2 miles or 0.3 km away)
- Savannah History Museum (0.24 miles or 0.4 km away)
- City Market (0.24 miles or 0.4 km away)

Policy on Pets:

- Animal pets are not allowed to stay in the hotel.

Wingate by Wyndham Savannah Airport

50 Sylvester C. Formey Dr, Savannah, GA 31408, United States
  Phone: +1 912-544-1180

If you want a dose of Southern hospitality right from getting off from your flight, then choose this hotel to stay at during your trip to Savannah. You can also either relax at the nearby leisure and entertainment locations, or head downtown for a historical tour of the city.

Highly Rated Amenities:

- Pick-up from and Drop-off at the Airport
- Free Public Parking Spaces
- Tour Desk
- Shuttle Service to Key Savannah Locations
- Free Wi-Fi in All Areas of the Hotel
- Swimming Pool
- Heated Pool
- Gym and Fitness Center
- Sun Terrace

Closest Airport:

- Savannah/Hilton Head International Airport (1.9 miles or 3.1 km away)

Nearby Landmarks and Tourist Spots:

- Traffic Circle Shopping Center (5.9 miles or 9.6 km away)
- Mary Galder Golf Course (6.6 miles or 10.6 km away)
- Jasper Spring (7.0 miles or 11.3 km away)
- Savannah National Wildlife Refuge (7.1 miles or 11.5 km away)

- Forsyth Park (8.6 miles or 13.9 km away)

Policy on Pets:

- No pets are allowed inside the hotel.

Research well, and book in advance to get the best discounts and packages from the hotel of your choice. Be sure as well to check out the reviews of actual hotel guests before making a reservation.

5

Best Famous Landmarks in the City

There are only a handful of cities in the United States that can match the storied beauty and charm of Savannah. To prove this, here are the best landmarks that attract millions of visitors into the city.

Bonaventure Cemetery

330 Bonaventure Rd, Thunderbolt, GA 31404, United States

It may seem odd that one of the top landmarks of a city include a cemetery, but this is what makes Savannah a unique tourist destination.

The haunting beauty of this cemetery has captured the imagination of writers and artists from different generations. This also serves as the final resting place for several prominent Savannah historical and influential figures, such as Gen. Hugo W. Mercer (1808-1877), and Pulitzer Prize winner Conrad Aiken (1899-1973).

In case you are in the mood for something other than the usual parks, then you should join the weekend tours on this cemetery.

Cathedral of St. John the Baptist

222 E Harris St, Savannah, GA 31401, United States

As the oldest Catholic church in Georgia, this mostly attracts those who are highly attuned with the faith and spirituality.

If you are not one of them, then you may still want to see this landmark for yourself to better appreciate the excellent workmanship that restored the church after a devastating fire in the early 20th century.

Inside the cathedral, you may view the large wooden Stations of the Cross that were imported from Germany and installed in 1900. There are also Austrian stained glass windows from the same period. Many also marvel at the 2,000-pound Noack pipe organ that remains functional up to this day.

Visitors may go around the cathedral every day from 09:00 to 05:00 PM. Pictures may be taken, except during a mass.

Fort Pulaski National Monument

24G5+RR Tybee Island, Georgia, United States

There is much more to do in the Tybee Island beside relaxing by the beach. Here, you will find the Fort Pulaski National Monument, a 19th century military post of the US Confederate Army.

History buffs may enjoy going to this landmark to get a better understanding of Savannah's role during the Civil War. There are also three cannon firing demonstrations held every Saturday—one at 11:00 AM, then at 01:00 PM, and finally at 03:00 PM.

Forsyth Park

2 W Gaston St, Savannah, GA 31401, United States

This is one of the most photographed landmarks in Savannah. Situated near the southern border of the Historic District, this park is made famous by its two-tiered cast-iron water fountain that was featured in the "Midnight in the Garden of Good and Evil", the best-selling work of John Berendt.

To see the park at its best, schedule your visit around the middle of March. At this time of the year, the azaleas would be in full bloom, and the fountain waters would be turned green in honor of St. Patrick's Day.

Remember to bring your camera with you to capture the beauty of this park. Other activities that may be done in the park include people-watching, picnics, various sports, and sun-bathing.

Savannah's Squares

Perhaps the best known landmark of Savannah is its collection of 22—originally 24—public squares in the Historic District.

Each one is named after important people or events in the history of Savannah. As such, you will find statues, tributes, and plaques honoring them. For your reference, here are the names of each square that remains in existence today:

1. Calhoun Square
2. Chatham Square
3. Chippewa Square
4. Columbia Square
5. Crawford Square
6. Ellis Square
7. Franklin Square

8. Greene Square
9. Johnson Square
10. Lafayette Square
11. Madison Square
12. Monterey Square
13. Oglethorpe Square
14. Orleans Square
15. Pulaski Square
16. Reynolds Square
17. Telfair Square
18. Troup Square
19. Warren Square
20. Washington Square
21. Whitefield Square
22. Wright Square

As mentioned earlier, two of the squares—Elbert Square and Liberty Square—have been removed from the list. Liberty Square has been sacrificed for the sake of the expansion of commercial spaces, while Elbert Square was damaged by a great fire in the 19th century.

Though the squares are located near one another, it may still take up a bit of your time to explore every one of them.

In that case, you should see first Monterey Square, which is considered as the most beautiful by locals and visitors alike. Then, walk north from there to go through the Madison, Chippewa Square, Wright Square, and Johnson Square. Each of these feature the best statues and monuments that every Savannah visitor must see.

As you can tell from this list, Savannah has sights to offer for nearly everybody. Whether you want to go for regular sight-seeing, or for something more macabre, there is a high chance that you will find something you would enjoy in the city.

Make sure to include these landmarks in your itinerary for your visit to the city. Again, most of these near the other tourist attractions of the city. Therefore, allotting some time to admire them should be no trouble at all.

6

Best Museums

As one of the earliest coastal towns in America, it is no surprise that Savannah is home to several important museums that cover a wide range of interests. There are also some contemporary museums that showcases the unique qualities of modern Savannah.

Whether you want to learn more about the history of Savannah, or you are simply interested in artifacts and legends, you would surely find something worth visiting in this list of the best museums in the city.

Savannah History Museum

303 Martin Luther King Jr Blvd, Savannah, GA 31401, United States
  +1 912-651-6825

For the history buffs, this museum may be the best source of information with regards to the role of Savannah during the American Revolution and the American Civil War.

It also highlights several cultural milestones and important points in the history of the city since its establishment in 1733.
  Opening Hours:

Daily – 09:00 AM to 05:00 PM

Telfair Academy of Arts and Museum

207 W York St, Savannah, GA 31401, United States
  +1 912-790-8800

First opened in 1886, this is the oldest public art museum in Southern America. Most of its collection are 19th and 20th American and European artworks created by gifted artists such as Childe Hassam and Frederick Frieseke.

The façade and structure of the museum itself is also a work of art. Carefully renovated by the descendants of Edward Telfair, the architecture continues to astound many of its visitors.

Opening Hours:

- Sunday to Monday – 12:00 NN to 05:00 PM
- Tuesday to Saturday – 10:00 AM to 05:00 PM

Ships of the Sea Maritime Museum

41 Martin Luther King Jr Blvd, Savannah, GA 31401, United States
   +1 912-232-1511

Up to this day, the Savannah River remains to be a major route for the ships and barges of all kinds. To highlight the importance and history of this river, this museum features several naval accounts and important aquatic feats that occurred in the Savannah River during the 18th and 19th centuries.

You may also find nautical paintings that depict these scenes, as well as artifacts and models of the nine most important ships that played significant roles throughout the early history of Savannah.

Opening Hours:

- Tuesday to Sunday – 10:00 AM to 05:00 PM
- Monday – Closed

Pin Point Heritage Museum

9924 Pin Point Ave, Savannah, GA 31406, United States
  +1 912-355-0064

This museum is all about celebrating the history and culture of the Gullah and Geechee communities of Pin Point, Savannah. These two ethnicities are the only African-American Creole groups that reside in Northern America.

The current structure of the museum served as the oyster and crab factory constructed by A.S. Varn & Son in the 20th century. After the factory has been formally closed in the 1980's, the community helped in turning this into a major historical and cultural hub of the city.

Opening Hours:

  · Thursday to Saturday – 09:00 AM to 05:00 PM
  · Sunday to Wednesday – Closed

Juliette Gordon Low Birthplace

10 E Oglethorpe Ave, Savannah, GA 31401, United States
  +1 912-233-4501

In case you are visiting Savannah with young kids in tow, then your group should stop by the Juliette Gordon Low Birthplace. This is a house museum that is dedicated for the life and achievements of the original founder of the American Girl Scouts—Juliette Gordon Low.

As the name suggests, Juliette was born in this house, where she also officially launched the Girl Scouts of America back in 1912.

To learn more about Juliette Gordon Low and the history of the of the American Girl Scouts, the museum offers a forty-minute guided tour for its guests.

Opening Hours:

- Monday to Saturday – 10:00 AM to 05:00 PM
- Sunday – Closed

Once you have gone through the above given list of highly recommended museums, you would gain a deeper insight on the history and culture of Savannah.

As you can see, it is not all about the Historic District. Savannah is rife with stories to tell, and the best way to experience them is through the museums all over the city. Try spending a day in your trip just soaking in these stories. By doing so, you might feel a deeper connection to the city and the people of Savannah themselves.

7

Best Art Galleries

Aside from its wide selection of art museums, Savannah is home to several private and community art galleries. The number comes as a surprise given the relatively small size of the city. The prevalence of art-related institutions may be attributed to the programs of the Savannah College of Art and Design, which promote the works of both new and established artists.

At some point, you might feel overwhelmed by the sheer volume of art galleries in the city. To figure out where you should go first, here are the best art galleries in Savannah:

A.T. Hun Art Gallery

302 W St Julian St, Savannah, GA 31401, United States
  +1 912-233-2060

Located at the City Market, this art gallery is known for its selection of eclectic and edgy artworks that are created by contemporary artists from Savannah and other parts of the world.

Opening Hours:

- Monday to Wednesday – 10:00 AM to 09:00 PM
- Thursday to Sunday – 10:00 AM to 10:00 PM

Gallery 209

209 E River St, Savannah, GA 31401, United States
  +1 912-236-4583

Gallery 209 is located in an old warehouse in a historic area. The gallery has a great art selection by local artists.

Opening Hours:

- Monday to Wednesday – 10:00 AM to 09:00 PM
- Thursday to Sunday – 10:00 AM to 10:00 PM

The Ray Ellis Gallery

3WJ4+37 Savannah, Georgia, United States
  +1 912-234-3537

This gallery is dedicated solely to the works of the great American painter, Ray Ellis. Even though he is not a Savannah homegrown talent, the locals have grown to love his artworks primarily due to his excellent depictions of the life in Southeast America.

Opening Hours:

- Monday to Wednesday – 10:00 AM to 09:00 PM
- Thursday to Sunday – 10:00 AM to 10:00 PM

Roots Up Gallery

412 Whitaker St c, Savannah, GA 31401, United States
  +1 912-677-2845

Overlooked artists find the recognition that they truly deserve in this gallery. Rather than promoting those who have already established themselves in the art world, this gallery aims to highlight the creativity of outsiders, and self-taught artists of Savannah and other nearby areas.

Aside from paintings, you may also peruse and purchase sculptures, fabrics, jewelry, and pottery—all of which are affordable for most tourists and locals.

Opening Hours:

- Tuesday to Saturday — 11:00 AM to 05:30 PM
- Sunday — 12:00 NN to 04:00 PM

Signature Gallery of Savannah

303 W St Julian St, Savannah, GA 31401, United States
 +1 912-233-3082

If you enjoy listening to the creative process of the artists as they made their masterpieces, then you should head over to this museum.

In here, you would get the chance to interact more closely with the other guests and the featured artists themselves.

Their selection is also not just limited to paintings, but also jewelry, glass works, pottery, and sculpture. Browse carefully through each one of them, and you may just find the perfect souvenir from Savannah.

Opening Hours:

- Monday to Wednesday — 10:00 AM to 09:00 PM
- Thursday to Sunday — 10:00 AM to 10:00 PM

You may browse through these art galleries at your own leisure, but to maximize the experience, you should consider going on organized art walks around Savannah. For example, the Second Saturday Art Walk holds monthly tours mostly in the galleries located at Downtown Savannah. Though you have to register in advance to join, the art walk is free for everyone.

8

Top 5 Restaurants

If you thought that all you can eat in Savannah are Southern fried foods, then you are sorely mistaken. Due to the city's proximity to the Atlantic coast, restaurants in Savannah are able to offer a wide variety of dishes that may delight even the pickiest eaters.

To experience Savannah cuisine at its best, here are the top 5 restaurants in the city that you should try:

Cotton & Rye

1801 Habersham St, Savannah, GA 31401, United States
  +1 912-777-6286

This is an upscale American restaurant that specializes in gourmet takes on classic Southern American cuisine.

Though they are mostly known for their James Beard Award-winning chicken wings, the restaurant elevates other dishes by preparing the bread, pickles, and charcuterie in the restaurant kitchen. In reference to its name, the freshly baked rye bread slices are served in a white cotton wrap.

Must-Try:

- Award Winning (For Real) Crispy Chicken Wings
- Sausage & Cheese Board
- Hanger Steak
- Stuffed Carolina Trout
- Beelers Pork Chop

Opening Hours:

- Monday to Saturday – 05:00 PM to 10:00 PM
- Sunday – Closed

Elizabeth on 37th

105 E 37th St, Savannah, GA 31401, United States
  +1 912-236-5547

First opened in 1981 by husband-and-wife duo Michael and Elizabeth Terry, this restaurant aims to showcase the best seafood harvested from the nearby coasts.

To compliment this, the chefs mainly use the herbs and edible flowers that are grown in their own garden. They also support the regional producers by incorporating into their dishes the fruits and vegetables that are also natives of the South.

Must-Try:

- Half-Moon River Clams
- Parmesan Dusted Local Flounder
- Spicy Savannah Red Rice with Georgia Shrimp
- Double-Cut Berkshire Pork Chop
- Fresh Fruit Pie

Opening Hours:

- Daily – 06:00 PM to 10:00 PM

Mrs. Wilkes Dining Room

107 W Jones St, Savannah, GA 31401, United States
  +1 912-232-5997

This restaurant is reminiscent of the traditional Southern boarding houses that offer communal dining experiences two times a day.

As such, the menu features home-style cooking of popular American comfort foods. To maintain its quality, Mrs. Wilkes, the proprietor, sources out her fruits and vegetables from the local farmers.

Must-Try:

- Fried Chicken
- Beef Stew
- Macaroni & Cheese
- English Peas & Noodles
- Candied Yams

Opening Hours:

- Monday to Friday – 11:00 AM to 02:00 PM
- Saturday & Sunday – Closed
- Entire Month of January – Closed

The Grey

109 Martin Luther King Jr Blvd, Savannah, GA 31401, United States
  +1 912-662-5999

What makes this restaurant unique is its structure—a restored art deco Greyhound bus terminal from the late 30's.

The steeper than average price of the food here is well worth every penny. To complete the experience, make sure to pair your order with the perfect drink from the selection of Atlantic Trade liquors and European wines that the restaurant offers.

Must-Try:

- Shrimp Ceviche
- Smoked Lamb
- Whole Fried Flounder
- Yard Bird
- Apple Tart

Opening Hours:

- Tuesday to Thursday – 04:00 PM to 11:00 PM
- Friday to Saturday – 12:00 NN to 12:00 MN
- Sunday – 12:00 NN to 10:00 PM

The Olde Pink House

23 Abercorn St, Savannah, GA 31401, United States
  +1 912-232-4286

Originally called the "Habersham House", this restaurant has earned its current name when the original white plastered walls of the house have been changed to Jamaican pink.

The history of the restaurant is just as rich as their menu. As such, be sure to try both their soulful dishes for the lunch menu and dinner menu.

Must-Try:

- Fish Taco
- Fried Chicken Livers
- Pan-Seared Jumbo Lump Crab Cake
- Crispy Half Duck
- Oyster on the Half Shell

Opening Hours:

- Lunch Menu
- Tuesday to Saturday — 11:00 AM to 02:30 PM
- Dinner Menu
- Sunday to Thursday — 05:00 PM to 10:30 PM
- Friday to Saturday — 05:00 PM to 11:00 PM

You may view the complete menu of these restaurants in their respective official websites. To guarantee your satisfaction, go through the reviews of locals and travelers who have dined already dined at these restaurants.

9

Best Coffee Shops

Savannah locals take their coffee shops to the next level. In fact, each shop seems to thrive through the collective effort of the community. Aside from supporting the regional coffee producers, Savannah coffee shops frequently feature several homegrown artists and musicians.

To satisfy your cravings for caffeine, here are the 5 best coffee shops in Savannah.

Foxy Loxy Café

1919 Bull St, Savannah, GA 31401, United States
  +1 912-401-0543

Your trip to Savannah is not complete without dropping by the Foxy Loxy Café—a coffee shop in Midtown, Savannah that sets itself apart from the rest by incorporating Tex-Mex cuisine into their menu.

Live music is hosted here every Tuesday, featuring mostly local musicians. If you enjoy the outdoors, bonfires are lit in its backyard every Saturday. They also offer a great selection of cheese boards, and Sunday brunch.

Must-Try:

- Mexican Mocha
- Horchata Latte
- Café Con Leche
- Kolache
- Foxy Scramble Burrito

Opening Hours:

- Monday to Saturday — 07:00 AM to 11:00 PM
- Sunday — 08:00 AM to 06:00 PM

The Coffee Fox

102 W Broughton St, Savannah, GA 31401, United States
  +1 912-401-0399

The success and popularity of the Foxy Loxy Café have led to the opening of The Coffee Fox—its sister coffee shop in downtown Savannah.

The menu of this coffee shop is mostly a condensed version of the Foxy Loxy Café, though there are some additions, such as the ones listed below, that stand out for many of its customers. Its main distinctions from its sister coffee shop are the humorous décor, quirky ambience, and stronger signature drinks they offer.

Must-Try:

- Cafe Au Lait
- Nitro Cold Brew Coffee
- Affogato
- Kolache
- Huevos Rancheros Quiche

Opening Hours:

- Monday to Wednesday – 07:00 AM to 09:00 PM
- Thursday to Saturday – 07:00 AM to 11:00 PM
- Sunday – 08:00 AM to 06:00 PM

The Foundery Coffee Pub

1313 Habersham St, Savannah, GA 31401, United States

This non-profit coffee shop—with its tagline "Coffee Cultivating Community" — supports various local initiatives, artists, and the United Methodist Church.

Though their selection of beverages is simpler than some of the popular coffee shops in Savannah, they make up for it in terms of the quality of their brews. The regulars though get to enjoy secret menu items that come with pop culture names and fun, quirky flavors.

The warehouse-like structure of the coffee shop also gives the customers plenty of room to hang out, work, or study.

Must-Try:

- Traditional Espresso Macchiatto
- Cubano
- Iced Latte
- Hot Chocolate
- Peach Tea

Opening Hours:

- Monday to Saturday — 07:00 AM to 10:00 PM
- Sunday — 09:00 AM to 09:00 PM

The Gallery Espresso

234 Bull St, Savannah, GA 31401, United States
+1 912-233-5348

This is a French-inspired coffee shop located right next to Chippewa Square in the heart of Savannah.

While getting your daily dose of caffeine, you may also browse through the various artworks of local artists that are featured inside the open-plan shop. They also have a great selection of cakes and pastries that go well with their house blends.

Must-Try:

- Gallery Espresso House Blend
- Freido
- Chai Tea
- Cheesecake
- Scones

Opening Hours:

- Monday to Friday – 07:30 AM to 10:00 PM
- Saturday to Sunday – 08:00 AM to 10:00 PM

Sentient Bean

13 E Park Ave, Savannah, GA 31401, United States
+1 912-232-4447

This coffee shop takes pride of their 100% organic and fair trade coffee. Furthermore, by bringing your own mug, you can get a small discount. If you prefer your coffee to-go, then you would have to pay a little bit more for their biodegradable wares.

Sentient Bean is also known for its vegetarian menu and gluten-free options. For entertainment, they host various performances in the evening, such as poetry readings, film screenings, and music shows.

Must-Try:

- Shot in the Dark
- Yerba Matte
- Frozen Mocha
- Heart of Gold
- Annie's Special Brunch

Opening Hours:

- Daily – 07:00 AM to 10:00 PM

There are several more coffee shops that you should try while you are in Savannah. Explore what the city has to offer, and you might just find your new favorite drink.

10

Top 5 Bars

Aside from historical and haunted sites, Savannah is also home to several iconic bars that deserve to be included in your itinerary. Discover below the best bars the city has to offer.

Churchill's Pub

13 W Bay St, Savannah, GA 31401, United States
  +1 912-232-8501

This is a British-owned and inspired pub that is famous for its wide selection of beers, cocktails, and wines.

To complement these drinks, you may choose to pair them with traditional British appetizers, entrees, and desserts. If you are in the mood for something American, however, then you are in luck because this pub also features contemporary American cuisine.

For those who want to hang out in a more intimate and relaxed scene, then you may opt to spend time in the lower level of the bar named the Winston's Wine Cellar. You may also book this for events and parties with your family and friends.

Opening Hours:

- Monday to Thursday – 05:00 PM to 11:00 PM
- Friday to Sunday – 05:00 PM to 12:00 MN

Jen's & Friends

34 Bull St, Savannah, GA 31401, United States
  +1 912-238-5367

Best known for being home to more than 200 beers and 300 martinis, this bar sets itself above and beyond the rest through the expertise of its owner and bartender, Jen McEvoy.

Though it may seem unassuming at first, with its neighborhood-style décor and chill vibes, this bar has proven time and again that is worthy of all the awards and recognition from both the locals and tourists.

Opening Hours:

- Monday to Wednesday – 03:00 PM to 12:00 MN
- Thursday – 03:00 PM to 01:00 AM
- Friday to Saturday – 03:00 PM to 02:00 AM
- Sunday – Closed

The Original Pinkie Masters

318 Drayton St, Savannah, GA 31401, United States
   +1 912-999-7106

As one of the longest running bar in Savannah, this local institution keeps the patrons coming back by reminding everyone of the good ol' days.

From its jukebox, to the various mementos from special events and high-profile guests, you would surely be thrown back in time, like when Jimmy Carter, as then governor of the state, first announced his candidacy for US presidency.

The cheap beer and gin cocktails also attract a wide variety of people, including art students, young professionals, and even those who come from influential families in Savannah.

Opening Hours:

- Monday to Saturday – 04:00 PM to 03:00 AM
- Sunday – Closed

The Distillery

416 W Liberty St, Savannah, GA 31401, United States
   +1 912-236-1772

Beer lovers will find paradise in this bar. Featuring more than 100 craft brews and 21 beer taps that rotate its selection of brews every night, The Distillery is a constant favorite for many locals and visitors.

In case you do not enjoy beer, then you may still enjoy yourself by ordering a drink from their selection of excellent wines, and fun cocktail specials.

The bartenders and servers of this bar are also trained and oriented well enough to help you find the right beverage for you. You may also ask for their recommendation on what food would go best with your selected drink.

Opening Hours:

- Sunday to Wednesday – 11:00 AM to 11:00 PM
- Thursday to Saturday – 11:00 AM to 12:00 MN

The Rail Pub

405 W Congress St #2410, Savannah, GA 31401, United States
   +1 912-238-1311

This pub comes with a rather interesting past. Since its opening in the latter part of 19th century, it has gone through several phases, most notably as a brothel.

Nowadays, this has turned into one of the most visited bars in Savannah. Many flock here for the customized cocktail drinks, karaoke machine, and its unique selection of bar snacks.

Opening Hours:

- Monday to Wednesday – 03:00 PM to 03:00 AM
- Thursday to Saturday – 01:00 PM to 03:00 AM
- Sunday – Closed

A true Savannah evening is not complete without a quick trip to the bar. Buy a round of drinks, if you are feeling extra generous, and the friendly crowd of locals would surely love you for it.

11

Top 5 Night Clubs

The nightlife in Savannah is thriving with loud music, strong drinks, and a lively crowd. You can find a lot of night clubs, particularly in the Historic District and nearby surrounding areas. To help you get into the right one that would fit with your vibe, here is a list of the five most recommended night clubs in Savannah.

Club 51 Degrees

121 W Congress St, Savannah, GA 31401, United States
+1 912-234-7265

This night club is known for playing different types of music for each of its three floors: hip-hop, Latin, and electronic. Of the three, the third floor has proven to be the most popular among the locals and tourists.

Remember to go to this club in your best outfit for club dancing. The bouncers here might turn you away if you would not follow this dress rule.

Opening Hours:

- Thursday to Saturday – 09:00 AM to 03:00 AM
- Sunday to Wednesday – Closed

Club 309 West

309 W River St, Savannah, GA 31401, United States
+1 912-236-1901

This club features two separate dancing halls—one for live bands, and the other one for DJs.

It mainly draws crowds, however, through their bartenders who dance on top of the bar, and their special promos for women guests.

Opening Hours:

- Wednesday – 10:00 PM to 03:00 AM

- Thursday to Saturday – 09:00 AM to 03:00 AM
- Sunday to Tuesday – Closed

Club One

1 Jefferson St, Savannah, GA 31401, United States
  +1 912-232-0200

Many people know this club as the home of Lady Chablis, one of the quirky real-life Savannah figures that appeared in the book "Midnight in the Garden of Good and Evil".

However, this night club has more to offer than their raunchy drag queens. Guests may indulge themselves in the 1,000-square-feet dance floor. Those who enjoy watching more than dancing themselves may be treated to cabaret performances.

This is also an LGBT-friendly night club. It is not open for credit card use, however, so make sure to bring cash or your ATM card with you.

Opening Hours:

- Monday to Saturday – 05:00 PM to 03:00 AM
- Sunday – 05:00 PM to 02:00 AM

Elan Savannah

301 Williamson St, Savannah, GA 31401, United States
  +1 912-662-3526

This night club also doubles as an event venue for both local and international touring acts.

As a night club, expect a lot of EDM (Electro Dance Music), though they also sometimes hold theme nights.

This is only one of the few night clubs in Savannah that accepts minors from ages 18 and up.

Opening Hours:

- Thursday – 10:00 PM to 3:00 AM
- Friday to Saturday – 09:00 PM to 03:00 AM
- Sunday to Wednesday – Closed

Saddle Bags Savannah

317 W River St, Savannah, GA 31401, United States
  +1 912-349-5275

If you want to spend the night in a country-themed night club, then this is the perfect choice for you.

Live country music stirs up the crowd to throw down, and some nights, the club offers free lessons on line dancing. Regulars could then begin line dancing whenever the mood struck them.

There is also a mechanical bull for those who enjoy being roughed up a bit. Head to the bar as well for a bourbon slush, a popular frozen alcoholic drink among its patron.

Opening Hours:

- Wednesday to Friday 04:00 PM to 03:00 AM
- Saturday – 12:00 NN to 03:00 AM
- Sunday – 12:00 NN to 02:00 AM

As with any night club, remember to be respectful of the staff and other guests. It is great to enjoy yourself, but try to do things in moderation.

12

List of Special Things You Can Only Do in Savannah

You will never get bored in Savannah—that is a guarantee. From its cuisine to its claim to fame, the city is filled of special things that are uniquely Savannah.

To save you from having to spend hours researching about things that you can do in this city, here is a rundown of the top 5 experiences that you can only have in Savannah.

Tease your palate through the Savannah Food Tour

Phone:1-800-987-9852

One of the best ways to get to know a place in a deeper level is through its food. You may visit the local restaurants in your own time, but that would entail a lot of research and planning from your own end.

To make things easier for visitors, the Savannah Food Tour offers a two-hour culinary tour aboard a bus around the Historic District.

The tour would stop by selected restaurants the offer samplers of Savannah cuisine offered in their respective menus. Though they are bite-sized only, try to pace yourself as much as possible. The number of stops in this tour might make it impossible for you to savor the last few samplers.

Head down to the Forsyth Farmers' Market

Every Saturday, a farmers' market opens at the south end of the Forsyth Park from 09:00 AM until 01:00 PM.

Here, you would be able to shop for locally grown produce and other goods, such as fresh herbs, coffee beans, sauces, cheese, and honey.

If you enjoy gardening, then you may take home with you a potted plant that is native only to Savannah.

Rain or shine, you may expect to see, and choose from a wide variety of Savannah foods and plants.

Take in the city while riding a horse-drawn carriage

Carriage Tours of Savannah

19 Jefferson St, Savannah, GA 31401, United States

+1 912-236-6756

If you want a rather authentic way of exploring the Historic District, indulge your adventurous side by going on a carriage tour.

This tour comes with real horses, and a coachman who would share stories and interesting facts about Savannah throughout the ride. These coachmen are locals, so you may them for tips on where you should go next, and their recommendations on the best eating spots in the city.

A carriage tour around Historic District lasts for about 50 minutes. You may bring along 5 more adults with you, but be sure to make a reservation at least 48 hours before your planned ride. Otherwise, you might end up wasting a good portion of your day in line for this tour.

Go shopping on Whitaker Street

Fashion enthusiasts can get their fill of unique finds in the Downtown Design District of Savannah. You may find these fashion boutiques along the Whitaker Street near the upper portion of the Forsyth Park.

Locals and tourists alike would find surely find something worth a space in their closets in shops like "One Fish Two Fish, and the "Custard Boutique".

Join the Night Ghost Tour

404 Abercorn St, Savannah, GA 31401, United States
  Phone: +1 912-292-0960

For thrill seekers and great believers of the unknown, the Night Ghost Tour of the Ghosts & Gravestones tour agency is a must-try.

Given that Savannah is considered by many as the most haunted city in the US, this tour that runs for a little over an hour seems to be keen on proving this claim.

On this tour, you would be able to visit historic cemeteries, former battle-grounds of past wars, and mansions built during the early days of the city. Stories and commentary accompany these sights to keep things lively and entertaining.

There is no shortage of unique things to do in Savannah. If your interests lie elsewhere from this list, then go out and explore the City Market and River Street. These iconic locations are home to various specialty shops and attractions that just might meet your expectations for a good time.

13

3-Day Travel Itinerary

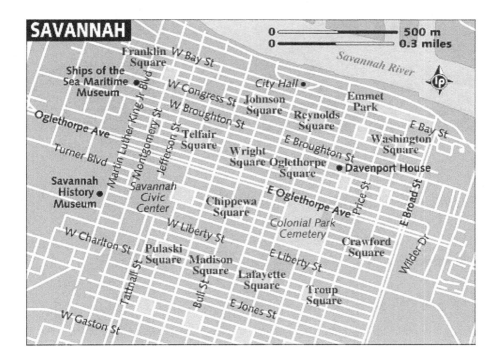

Are you planning to spend an extended weekend in Savannah? Or perhaps, you and your family have been putting this trip off because you cannot seem to agree on the schedule of events?

To save you from these hassles and more, here is a sample 3-day travel itinerary for a trip to Savannah.

Day 1 - Kick things off with a bang!

Objective: To visit the best of Savannah

Places to Visit:

- City Market
- Forsyth Park
- The Cathedral of St. John the Baptist
- Savannah Foody Tour

Grab a Bite:

- Leopold's
- Foxy Loxy
- Jen's & Friends

Fun Things to Do:

- Go square–hopping across the Historic District.
- Take pictures at Forsyth Park.

Day 2 – Discover the different sides of Savannah

Objective: To deepen your understanding of the history and culture of the city

Places to Visit:

- Savannah History Museum
- Telfair Academy of Arts and Museum
- Ships of the Sea Maritime Museum
- The Owens-Thomas House
- Juliette Gordon Low Birthplace

Grab a Bite:

- The Gallery Espresso
- The Olde Pink House
- Cotton & Rye

Fun Things to Do:

- Watch a performance or see a film in the Historic Savannah Theater.
- Dance the night away in Club One.

Day 3 – Explore more

Objective: To widen the scope of your tour beyond your comfort zone

Places to Visit:

- Wormsloe Historic Site
- Pin Point Heritage Museum
- Fort Pulaski National Monument
- Bonaventure Cemetery
- Old Fort Jackson Historic Site
- Colonial Park Cemetery

Grab a Bite:

- Mrs. Wilkes' Dining Room
- The Rail Pub

Fun Things to Do:

- Attend a cannon-firing demonstration at Fort Pulaski.
- Go on a Savannah Night Ghost Tour.

There is so much to do in a city that is as historically and culturally rich as Savannah. This three-day itinerary is just an overview of everything that the city has to offer.

Keep in mind that you also do not have to follow this itinerary to the letter.

If you have something worth doing or a place worth visiting, then consider listening to your intuition. It would be best though if you could keep the structure and objectives for each day so that you can have a fulfilling and exciting trip to Savannah.

After you have gone on this trip, feel free to return to the city, and check out the things that you have missed on your first run. Next time, consider bringing along your family and friends with you. Based on what you have learned from this guide, you can now better introduce them to the wonders of this Southern city.

Conclusion

I'd like to thank you and congratulate you for transiting my lines from start to finish.

I hope this book was able to help you to learn everything you need to know about visiting Savannah.

The next step is to find the best deals for your flight, hotel stay, and tour packages. Set aside an hour or two for this in order to fully explore the options available at the moment.

Keep in mind the timing of your trip because, as explained earlier, this would affect the costs of your travel, and the activities that you may expect to do while you are in the city.

I wish you the best of luck!

Copyright

trademarks and brands within this book are for clarifying purposes only and are the owned by the owners themselves, not affiliated with this document.

Made in the USA
Monee, IL
23 July 2025

21727103R00062